The Sayings of Ibn Qayyim al-Jawziyyah (1292 – 1350 CE)

Ikram Hawramani

2017
STEWARDS PUBLISHING

STEWARDS PUBLISHING

COPYRIGHT © 2017-2018 IKRAM HAWRAMANI

FIRST EDITION OF 2017 – REVISION 2018-A

HAWRAMANI.COM

ALL RIGHTS RESERVED. NO PART OF THIS PUBLICATION MAY BE REPRODUCED, STORED IN A RETRIEVAL SYSTEM, OR TRANSMITTED, IN ANY FORM OR BY ANY MEANS FOR COMMERCIAL PURPOSES WITHOUT PRIOR PERMISSION OF THE AUTHOR. THE AUTHOR AFFIRMS THE READERS' RIGHT TO SHARE THIS BOOK FOR PERSONAL, NON-COMMERCIAL PURPOSES.

A Brief Biography of Ibn Qayyim al-Jawziyyah

Ibn al-Qayyim[1] was born in Damascus on January 28th of the year 1292 CE, equivalent to the seventh of Ṣafar of the year 691 AH. His full name is Abū ʿAbd-Allah Shams al-Dīn Muḥammad bin Abī Bakr al-Zuraʿī. His surname of Al-Zuraʿī refers to Zuraʿ, a village close to Damascus where his family comes from. He is known as Ibn al-Qayyim, which means "Son of the Principal", as a reference to the fact that his father Abū Bakr was the principal of the Jawzīya madrasa in Damascus.

Ibn Kathīr says about Ibn al-Qayyim: "I do not know in our time a person who spends more time in worship than he does." His student Ibn Ḥajar al-ʿAsqalānī says regarding him: "He used to sit after praying the *fajr* prayer until the sun rose high in the sky. He used to say 'This is my breakfast. If I ignore it, I will lose my strength.'" He also used to say 'Only through patience and *yaqīn* (heartfelt faith) can one attain leadership in the *dīn* (religion)'".

---

[1] Due to the peculiarities of the Arabic language, the correct way to refer to Ibn al-Qayyim is either as Ibn al-Qayyim or, if the full name is given, Ibn Qayyim al-Jawzīya (notice the missing "al" before "Qayyim"). In the book's title the last name of al-Jawziyyah was used due to the fact that this is a popular spelling; the standard academic transliteration, however, is al-Jawzīya.

Ibn al-Qayyim is one of the most important thinkers and writers of the Ḥanbalī school of jurisprudence and theology. Besides numerous scholarly works, he wrote a lengthy commentary on *Manāzil al-Sā'irīn* (*Stations of the Wayfarers*) by the major Iranian-Arab Sufi leader Khwaja Abdullah Ansari, which he titled *Madārij al-Sālikīn* (*Steps of the Pursuers*). Ibn al-Qayyim expresses his love for Ansari and in another work refers to him as Shaykh al-Islām (an honorific that means "the Sheikh of all Muslims").

Ibn al-Qayyim died in Damascus on September 15, 1350 CE, equivalent to the 13th of Rajab 751 AH. His funeral prayer was performed after the *ẓuhr* prayer at the Umayyad Mosque, attended by a very large crowd of scholars, officials and laypeople.

The Sayings of
Ibn Qayyim al-Jawziyyah

From Ten of His Books

This page intentionally left blank

I

Supplication (*duʿāʾ*) is one of the most powerful tools for countering misfortune and attaining what is sought, but its effects may be delayed, either because of a weakness in the supplicator's soul, by it being a prayer that God does not love due to it containing malicious intentions, or due to the weakness of the heart and it being turned away from God, or due to not being fully focused on God during the time of the supplication, so that it is like a bow whose string is not taut, or due to the occurrence of that which prevents the answering of the supplication, such as the consumption of the unlawful and the soul being overrun by sins.

2

A supplication made during adversity has three ranks: Either the supplication is stronger than the adversity so that it fully counters it, or that it is weaker than the adversity so that the adversity dominates and the supplicator ends up suffering from the adversity and not escaping it, though the supplication can weaken the adversity even if it is a weak supplication. And the third is that they are equal and cancel each other out.

3

Of the most beneficial cures is relentlessness in supplication and its opposite is for the servant to be hasty and for the answer to be delayed so that his heart breaks and he gives up supplication.

4

We often find supplications that a people used and which were answered by God. Such supplications are either coupled with the desperate need of the supplicant and his focus on God, or a good deed he had done in the past and for whose reward God answered the supplication, or the supplication was done at a time of answering [at a time when God willed to answer prayers], so that his prayer was answered. But people mistakenly think that the secret is in the phrasing of the supplication; they adopt it without considering the other conditions that were necessary for it to be answered.

5

The most arrogant of people is the one who lets himself be deceived by the worldly life and its immediate rewards, who prefers it to the Hereafter, and who has become content with it as a substitute for the Hereafter.

6

The servant continues to commit sins as long as they appear small in his eye and feel unimportant in his heart, and this is the sign of falling into disaster, for the smaller a sin is in the eyes of the servant the greater it is in the sight of God.

7

Do not consider God's saying "the righteous will be in bliss, and the wicked will be in a fire" to only apply to the bliss and torment of the Hereafter.

And is bliss other than the bliss of the heart, and is torment other than the torment of the heart?

8

Whoever loves something other than God will be tormented by it three times in this world: He will be tormented by its lack before he acquires it, and once he acquires it he is tormented by the fear of losing it [...] and when he loses it, his torment increases further.

9

The farther the heart is from God, the quicker it receives affliction, and the closer the heart is to God, the farther affliction will be from it. Distance from God comes in grades, some of which are more severe than others. The heart is like a bird; the more it ascends, the more distant it will be from affliction, and the more it descends, the more it is attacked by affliction.

10

God did not make this enemy[2] dominant over his faithful servant, who is among His most beloved creatures, except because of the fact that struggle in His cause is the most beloved thing in His eyes, and those who carry out this struggle have the highest ranks and regard in His eyes.

---

[2] Probably referring to the Mongols.

II

Nothing preserves the available blessings of God and begets the missing ones like obedience to Him, for what is with God cannot be gained except through His obedience.

12

The sound heart is the one that is safe from polytheism, malevolence, grudges, envy, greed and arrogance and the love of the worldly life and of mastery over others, so that it is safe from every affliction that can distance it from God, and from every form of confusion that would keep it from the knowledge of God, and from every desire that would go against his Lord's commands. God praises His Close Friend[3] for the soundness of his heart when He says: "And among [Noah's] kind was Abraham, When he came to his Lord with a sound heart" [Quran 37:83-84], and God also mentions Abraham saying: "The Day when there will not benefit [anyone] wealth or children, except one who comes to God with a sound heart." [Quran 26:88-89].

---

[3] *Khalīl*, one of the titles of Prophet Ibrāhīm.

13

Yaḥyā bin Muʿādh says: "The hearts are like containers, they overflow with what they contain, and the tongues are the edges of the containers." Therefore look at the person when he speaks and you will hear his tongue overflow with the contents of his heart, be they sweet or sour.

14

Thankfulness is built on three foundations: Acknowledgment of the blessing in one's heart, acknowledgement of the blessing in public, and the use of the blessing in accordance with the wishes of the Giver of the blessing.

15

True patience is to withhold the ego from vengeance when one has the ability to carry it out, to withhold the tongue from complaining, and to withhold the limbs from sinning.

16

The wisdom in God's afflicting His servant with hardship is that He did not afflict him to destroy him, but to test his patience and obedience.

17

The majority of people only carry out their duty of obedience only in things they like, even though the higher status belongs to carrying out the duty in things they dislike[4], since it is through these that the ranks of the servants are distinguished, and it is according to this that their degrees are decided in the sight of God.

---

[4] For example helping someone whom we do not like, or performing acts of worship that we do not particularly enjoy solely to please God.

18

God has made a judgment that cannot be undone or countered: That whoever loves anything other than Him will surely be tormented by it, and whoever fears other than Him will be subjected to that which he fears, and whoever busies himself with other than Him will be a cause of sadness and misfortune for him, and whoever prefers others to Him will see God's blessings taken out of what he does.

19

Satan has two ways of corrupting whatever God has commanded: Either through causing negligence, or through causing excessiveness and immoderation. He does not care through which of these he prevails over the servant.

20

Giving charity has a wonderful effect in removing various types of affliction, even if it comes from a great sinner or oppressor, and even if it comes from a disbeliever, for through it God removes many types of afflictions, and this is a matter well-known to people, the elite and the laypeople, and the people of earth all agree with it since it fits their experience.

21

Generosity is two types. The superior type is your needlessness for what others have, and the second is to spend of what you have. A man can be among the most generous of people without giving them anything, by being feeling toward what they have and never looking at what they have with the eye of greed and desire.

22

The heart acquires rust through heedlessness and sins, and it is polished by the seeking of forgiveness and the remembrance of God.

23

I heard Shaykh al-Islām Ibn Taymīya[5] saying: "On earth there is a paradise: whoever does not enter it, he will not enter Paradise in the afterlife". And he said to me: "What can my enemies do to me? I have my own paradise and orchard in my chest: if I leave this place, it stays with me and does not leave me. If they kill me, it will be martyrdom, and if they turn me out from my country, it will be tourism and sightseeing for me". He used to say in his *sujūd* ["prostration"] when he was imprisoned: "Oh God aid me in remembering You, thanking You and worshiping You in the best manner

---

[5] Ibn Taymīya (1263 – 1328 CE) is controversial today due to the use and abuse of his thought by extremist groups. Recent scholarship shows that he was a more balanced, moderate and sophisticated thinker than is realized by extremists. See Shahab Ahmed and Yossef Rapoport, *Ibn Taymiyya and His Times*, Karachi: Oxford University Press, 2017; Yahya Michot, *Ibn Taymiyya: Against Extremisms*, Beirut: Dar Albouraq, 2012.

possible." And he once told me: "the imprisoned one is the one whose heart is imprisoned away from his Lord".

24

The best remembrance [*dhikr*] is the one that is done simultaneously by the heart and the tongue. Remembrance by the heart alone is better than remembrance by the tongue alone, for the remembrance of the heart gives fruit to knowledge, polishes one's love [for God], increases modesty, creates fear [of God], and calls toward mindfulness, and it prevents negligence in acts of worship and trivialization of sins and evil deeds. Remembrance by the tongue alone does not bear those fruits, and if it bears fruit at all it will be very little.

25

Remembrance of God is better than supplication, because remembrance is the praising of God by His Beautiful Attributes, His Signs and His Names, while supplication is the servant's asking for his needs, so how can they be compared? The supplication that comes after remembrance and praise of God is better and more likely to be answered than a supplication by itself, and if the servant adds to his supplication a sincere description of his situation and acknowledgment of his desperate need for God, this would be better and it would increase his chance of having his prayer answered.

26

Is seeking God's forgiveness sufficient for repentance from *ghayba* ["backbiting"], or should the injured person be informed and forgiveness sought from him? There are two opinions among scholars on this matter, and the correct one is that there is no need to inform the person. It is sufficient to pray to God for the forgiveness of the person and to mention the person with good words in the place where he was backbitten before, and this is the choice if Shaykh al-Islām Ibn Taymīya.

27

When God says: "But perhaps you hate a thing and it is good for you; and perhaps you love a thing and it is bad for you. And God Knows, while you know not" [Quran 2:216], in this verse there are a number of secrets of wisdom and benefits for the servant. When the servant knows that what he hates may bring him what he loves, and what he loves may cause him what hates, he does not take his own happiness for granted and does not become proud, knowing that what makes him happy now can bring him misery in the future, and he does not despair when he is afflicted, knowing that since he does not know the consequences of all things, the affliction may bring him happiness in the future.

28

An important piece of wisdom: Refusing to perform a commandment is a greater sin than doing what you have been commanded not to do. The sin of doing what you have been commanded not to do is often due desire and need, while the sin of refusing to perform a commandment often originates from arrogance and self-glorification.

Sahl bin 'Abd-Allāh said: "Abandonment of carrying out commandments is greater in the sight of God than committing prohibited acts, for Adam was prohibited from eating from the tree but he did so and God forgave him, while Satan was commanded to prostrate to Adam and he refused to do so and God did not forgive him."

29

The righteous way of dealing with God's blessings is to first recognize and acknowledge them, and then to seek refuge in Him from attributing these blessings to other than Him even if there are material reasons for a blessing, because He is the ultimate initiator and maintainer of the blessing. All blessings originate from Him. The next step in dealing with God's blessings is to praise Him and love Him for them and to show gratitude toward Him by using these blessings in His obedience.

30

The best means of coming closer to God is to steadfastly follow the *sunna* in hidden and public deeds, to always be needful of God, and to solely desire Him and His approval through one's words and actions. No one can reach God except through these three, and no one is blocked from God except by abandoning these or one of them.

31

When God wants good for a servant, He causes him to acknowledge and confess his own sins and stops him from concerning himself with the sins and faults of others. He makes him generous of what he has, while making him ascetic toward what others have, and he makes him patient upon being hurt by others. While if He wants evil for a servant, He causes the opposite of these to him.

32

Contentment is the heart's serenity toward the flow of the decrees [of God].[6]

---

[6] It is to accept whatever happens in our lives without anger, disappointment or wishing things to be otherwise.

33

The most beneficial things to the *nafs* [the ego] are the things it dislikes, the same way that the most harmful and destructive things to it are the things it loves.

34

The decrees God makes about His servant [i.e. the blessings and calamities He sends] are always from [God's] justice, bounty, wisdom, and mercy, and they are never from anything other than these.

35

Every person is programmed to not abandon an immediate benefit and pleasure for a future benefit and pleasure that is out of sight and has to be waited for—unless he clearly sees the superiority of the future benefit over the immediate one and his desire is strong for the higher and better thing. If he prefers the imperfect and ephemeral benefit, it is either because he does not clearly see that it is inferior to something else, or because he has no desire for the superior benefit, and either of these cases shows a weakness of faith, mind and insight.

A person who prefers the worldly life either does believe that there is something better and more lasting, or does not believe. If he does not believe that there is anything better, he is without faith in his heart, and if he believes that there is something better but does not prefer it over the worldly life, it is because his mind is corrupt and he chooses wrongly for himself.

36

A servant is not afflicted with a punishment more severe than the hardness of the heart and distance from God.

If the hearts become hard, the eyes become dry [they no longer shed tears out of love or fear of God].

37

Hearts that are attached to pleasures are blocked from God by the amount of their attachment to pleasures. Hearts are God's goblets on earth. The most beloved of them to Him are the most delicate, the firmest and the most transparent among them.

38

Whoever wants a pure heart, then let him prefer God to his desires.

39

The longing for God and for meeting Him is a breeze that blows across the heart, removing from it the glittering illusions of the worldly life.

40

Following one's desires and putting one's hopes in the worldly life are the substances of every form of corruption.

41

The best thing that the souls can earn and the hearts can acquire and through which the servant can earn greatness in this world and the afterlife is knowledge and faith, and it is for this reason that God compared between them in His saying: "And those who were given knowledge and faith will say: You remained the extent of God's decree until the Day of Resurrection" [Quran 30:56] and His saying "God will raise those who have faith among you and those who were given knowledge, by degrees" [Quran 58:11]. Those are the chosen of the creation and its elite and are those who are eligible for the highest ranks.

42

Ibn Sīrīn says: "I heard Shurayḥ[7] swearing by God that whoever leaves something for God will find something else that he is missing". And the saying is true that whoever leaves something for the sake of God, God will give him a better substitute for it.

---

[7] Shurayḥ al-Kindī, a famous judge in the city of Kufa in Iraq who became Muslim during the Prophet's lifetime, peace be upon him, but who never met him.

43

Worshipping God through His blessings means for the smallest of His blessings to seem great in the eye of the servant, and for His great blessings to be equaled by his gratitude toward Him for them, and for him to know that the blessing reached him from his Master without any price that he paid for it and without any means that could guarantee his acquiring the blessing and without him deserving it, and in truth the blessing belongs to God, not to the servant, and through these realizations God's blessings only increase the humility, meekness, self-abasement and love of the servant toward the Giver, and whenever a blessing is renewed for him, it causes in him further obedience, love, humility and self-abasement toward God.

44

Whoever abandons [worrying about] choosing and planning for gain or out of fear of loss, or for health or out of fear of illness, and knows that God is All-Capable, that He alone has the true power of choice and planning, and that His planning for his servant is better than the servant's own planning for himself, and that He knows what is in the servant's interests better than the servant, and that He is more capable of securing those interests, and that He is a better guide to the servant than the servant, and that He is more merciful toward the servant than he is toward himself, and that He is more dutiful and loyal toward him than he is toward himself...once he throws himself into His arms like a weak servant in the hands of an All-Powerful King who can do anything He wills toward him, feeling utterly powerless and choiceless, his mind attains peace from worries, fears, melancholy and sorrows.

45

Do not let it appear overly difficult to go against society and join the side of God and His Prophet, even if you are alone by yourself, since you are under His gaze, His guardianship and protection, and He is only testing your faith and patience. Your best helpers in these after God is to be free from greed and fear. When you are free from them, it becomes trivially easy to stay with the side of God and His Prophet, and you will always be on the side where God and His Prophet are.

46

True asceticism is to abandon what has no benefit for the Hereafter, and true fear of God is to abandon what one fears will harm him in the Hereafter.

47

When the servant believes in the Scripture and acquires guidance through the whole of it and wholeheartedly accepts its commandments and believes in the information contained therein, this becomes the cause of another state of guidance that he ultimately acquires. Guidance has no end regardless of how well-guided the servant is, for as he continues to fear his Lord, he is promoted to a higher rank. God says: "Indeed, those who have believed and done righteous deeds—their Lord will guide them because of [or through] their faith" [Quran 10:9], thus He first guided them to faith, then after they became faithful, He guided them to another state of faith, guidance after guidance. A similar saying is His saying: "God increases those who were guided, in guidance" [Quran 19:76] and "O you who have believed, if you fear God, He will grant you a criterion" [Quran 8:29]. The criterion includes the light that He gives them with which they can distinguish between truth and falsehood, and the help and might with which they can uphold truth and break falsehood.

48

Sincerity and the desire for praise and the desire for that which is with people cannot be united together in the same heart any more than water and fire can be united.

49

If your soul desires that you seek sincerity, then first start by attacking greed and slaying it with the knife of despair [reach a state of complete loss of desire for worldly things], and attack the love for praise by becoming an ascetic toward it the way that the lovers of the worldly life are ascetic toward the Hereafter. If you succeed in slaying greed and becoming ascetic toward praise, sincerity will become easy for you.

50

Among the signs of success and blessedness are that the servant, as his knowledge increases, with it his humility and mercy increase, and as his good deeds increase, his fear and caution [of the Hereafter] increases, and as his age increases, his desire for worldly things decreases, and as his wealth increases, his generosity and charity increase, and as his status and power increase, he becomes closer to the common people, takes care of their needs and acts humbly toward them.

51

Of the signs of accursedness are that the servant, as his knowledge increases, his arrogance and pride increase, and as his good deeds increase, his pride in himself and his opinion of himself increase and he looks down on others, and as his age increases, his greed increases, and as his wealth increases, he becomes stingier, and as his power and status increase, his arrogance and pride increase.

52

There is nothing as harmful to the servant as his becoming bored with the blessings that God has bestowed over him, so that he no longer sees them as blessings, and he does not thank Him for them and is not pleased by them, but rather, he curses them and complains about them and considers them burdens and misfortunes.

53

Of the greatest oppression and ignorance is to seek glorification and honor from the people while your heart is empty of glorifying and honoring God.

54

The servant stands between the hands of God twice: When he is performing *ṣalāh* [the formal prayer], and when he stands before Him on the Day of Judgment. Whoever carries out the rights of the first standing properly, the second standing will be easy for him, and whoever does not take the first standing seriously and does not give it what is due to it, the second standing will be difficult for him.

55

God's saying that "there is not a thing but that with Us are its treasuries [or stores, or depositories]" [Quran 15:21] contains a treasure of wisdom, which is that a thing is not sought except from the one who controls its supply and has the keys to the container that contains it. If the thing is sought from someone else, they will not have it and will not be able to procure it.[8]

---

[8] In other words, since God controls the treasuries of all things, all things should primarily be sought from Him.

56

If people feel rich and needless through the worldly life, feel rich and needless through God, and if people are happy and pleased with the worldly life, let your happiness and pleasure be through God, and if they find peace and comfort in their loved ones, find peace and comfort in God, and if they know their kings and rulers and approach them to acquire glory and greatness, know God and become closer to Him to acquire the pinnacle of glory and greatness.

57

The worldly life is a rotten corpse. Lions do not attack rotten corpses.

58

Whoever resides his heart with his Lord finds peace and comfort, and whoever sends his heart out to be among the people finds worry and anxiety. The love of God does not enter a heart in which there is the love of the worldly life except the way that the camel enters the eye of a needle.

59

If God loves a servant, He prepares him for Himself and adopts Him for His love and chooses Him to dedicate his energies to worshiping Him.

60

By the amount that one desires the worldly life and seeks its approval, one will be unwilling to obey God and seek the Hereafter.

61

The ignorant one complains about God to the people. This is the height of ignorance about the one complained about and the one complained to, because had he known his Lord, he would not have complained about Him, and had he known the people, he would not have complained to them. One of the pious predecessors saw a man complaining to another man about his poverty and needfulness and said: "You! by God, what you have done is nothing more or less than complaining about one who has mercy and kindness for you to one who has none."

62

Remembrance of the sweetness of reaching your destination makes your struggle to get there easier and more bearable.

63

Stay cautious of your ego. No trial has afflicted you except through it. Do not make peace with it, for by God, no one can bring honor to it except one who has humiliated it, and no one can bring greatness to it except one who has made it insignificant and submissive, and no one can make it whole except one who has broken it, and no one can bring rest to it except one who has exhausted it, and no one can bring security to it except one who has frightened it, and no one can bring happiness to it except one who has brought sadness to it.

64

By God, no enemy can attack you except after your Protector has turned away from you. Do not think that Satan has won [when you feel weak in faith and overpowered], it is just that the Guardian has left [you].[9]

---

[9] It is your relationship with God that determines your ability to fight evil impulses.

65

O one who spends the commodity of his lifetime in going against the wishes of his Beloved and distancing himself from Him, there is not among your enemies one who does more harm to you than yourself.

66

A person who repents from a sin is like a sick person who drinks medicine, and perhaps an illness will be the cause of health.[10]

---

[10] In some cases to have sinned and then repented would bring better fruits to the servant than not having sinned at all.

67

Zayd bin Aslam[II] used to say: "Whoever fears God, the people will love him despite themselves".

[II] A Successor, scholar and hadith transmitter from Medina (d. 136 AH / 753-754 CE).

68

When those blessed with insight see the small value of the worldly life, its shortness, and the smallness of the value of one's status in it, they cause their desire for it to die out of their desire for the eternal life. When they wake up from the sleep of heedlessness, they work hard to recover what the enemy has robbed from them during their period of idleness, and when the road seems too long, they glance at the destination, so that it appears near to them, and whenever the worldly life commands them, they find sweetness in remembering "this is your Day which you have been promised" [Quran 21:103].

69

Whoever loses his peace among the people but finds it in solitude, he is true in faith, but weak. Whoever finds peace among the people but loses it in solitude, he has a sickness [of the heart]. And whoever has lost peace both when in solitude and when among the people, then he is dead and expelled [from God's presence]. And whoever finds peace both when in solitude and when among the people, he is the true lover [of God], the one who is strong in his condition. Whoever finds increase in his spirituality when in solitude, he cannot increase it except in solitude, and whoever finds increase when among the people, his increase can only be by them through giving them guidance and good advice. Whoever finds increase in carrying out God's desire regardless of where He puts him to use, he will find increase both in solitude and among the people, thus the highest status and the best condition is for you to not choose for yourself a condition except that which He chooses for you and puts you in; stay with what He desires for you to do, rather than with what you desire of Him to do for you.

70

There is no wonder in a servant humbling himself before God, worshiping Him and not tiring of worshiping him, when he has such a strong need and poverty toward Him. What is wondrous is a Master who loves His servant with the range and variety of His blessings and shows tenderness toward him with various types of kindness toward him even though He is perfectly needless of him:

It is sufficient honor for you that you are His servant

And it is sufficient pride for you that He is your Lord

71

Return to God and seek Him with your eyes, your ears, your heart and your tongue, and do not let these four wander away from Him, for no one is able to return to Him except through these four, and no one has wandered away from Him except by misusing one of these.

72

The land of human nature is wide and capable of growing whatever is planted in it. If you plant the tree of faith and fear of God, you will inherit the sweetest fruit, while if you plant the tree of ignorance and lust, all the fruit will be bitter.

73

Whoever is prevented from sinning by feeling the greatness of God's status in his heart, God increases his status in the hearts of the creation so that they do not belittle or dishonor him.

74

When Adam sought immortality in Paradise through the tree [rather than through God], he was punished by being cast out from it, and when Yusuf sought to get out of prison through the one who had seen the dream [rather than through God], he stayed in prison for a number of years.

75

When you fear the creation, you become paranoid and run away from them. But when you fear the Lord Almighty, you find peace in Him and move closer to Him.

76

How can one be sensible who sells Paradise with all that it contains for the pleasure of an hour?

77

The worldly life from its beginning to its end is not worth an hour's sorrow.

78

Reflect upon the words of the Quran and you will see a King to Whom belongs all dominion and to Whom all praise is due. The reins of all matters and affairs are in His hands, they originate from Him and find their conclusion through Him. He is established upon the seat of His kingdom, nothing is hidden from Him in any region of His domain. He is All-Knowing about what is in the hearts of His servants, knowing their secrets and what they show publicly. He alone has the power to manage the affairs of the kingdom; He hears and He sees, He gives and He withholds, He rewards and He punishes, He honors and He humiliates, He creates, gives sustenance, causes death, causes life, grants and arranges. All matters come from Him, the smallest and the greatest, and all matters find their conclusion with Him; they do not move by the amount of an atom except by His permission, and no leaf falls except that He has knowledge of it.

79

Whoever truly actualizes the meaning of *al-Fātiḥa*[12] through knowledge, recognition, and action and through his condition, he has won the best share of its perfection, and his worship has become the worship of the chosen elite whose ranks are high above those of the ordinary worshipers.

---

[12] The opening chapter of the Quran.

80

Of the attributes of the people of Paradise: "and [he] came with a heart returning [to God in repentance]" [Quran 50:33]. Ibn ʿAbbās said: "He returned from sinning against God to eager obedience". True return is for the heart to work on God's obedience, love, and eager striving toward Him. God then mentions the reward of those who had these attributes in His saying: "Enter it in peace, this is the day of immortality. For them is what they desire, and with us is ever more [to give to them]". [Quran 50:34-35]

81

Of the attributes of the people of Paradise: "Who feared the Most Gracious unseen [i.e. without seeing God, or in solitude without being seen by others]" [Quran 50:33].

82

When the servant sees that his forelock and the forelocks of all other servants are in the hands of God, steering them where He wishes, he will stop fearing them, wishing things from them, or putting them on pedestals, but will see them as dominated and mastered servants. When he sees himself like this, his poverty and needfulness toward God become a required attribute of his existence. And when he sees people in this way, he will stop feeling needful toward them and will not put his hope and expectations in them. In this way his monotheism, reliance and servitude become true and sincere.

83

The heart cannot be dedicated to the love of God unless it is emptied of the love of other than God. The heart's receptive ability is like the ear's; if it listens to other than the speech of God, it becomes incapable of receiving God's words, and if it inclines toward the love of other than God, it will lose its inclination for the love of God.

84

If knowledge without deeds had benefit, God wouldn't have condemned the clerics of the People of the Book, and if deeds without sincerity had benefit, God wouldn't have condemned the hypocrites.

85

The servant does not take what is forbidden from him except due to two things: Either he thinks wrongly of his Lord—he thinks that if he obeys Him and gives preference to Him He will not give him a better non-prohibited thing. The second one is that he knows that if someone leaves something for the sake of God, God will give him something better in its place, but his patience is overcome by his lust and his desire has overrun his brain. The first one is due to the weakness of his knowledge, the second one due to the weakness of his sense and insight.

86

Deeds without sincerity and without following the example of other righteous people is like a traveler filling his water bottle with dirt, which burdens him without benefiting him.

87

Whoever, among the workers, wishes to know his status in the eye of the King, let him look at what jobs He gives him and with what He busies him.

88

Whoever truly knows his own ego will be too busy working on fixing and improving it to concern himself with people's faults.

89

All sins are based on three things: Arrogance, which caused Satan to be the way he is; greed, which is what caused Adam to be cast out of Paradise, and envy, which is what pushed one of the sons of Adam to kill the other.

90

God joins guidance with struggle in His saying "as for those who strive in Our cause, We shall surely guide them to Our ways". The most perfect among the people when it comes to guidance are those who struggle the most in His cause, and the most obligatory struggle is the struggle against the ego and against desires, and the struggle against Satan and against the worldly life.

91

If the servant awakens in the morning and goes to sleep at night with his entire concern being God's pleasure, God will carry for him all his burdens and will carry out for him all his needs, and He will take away from him all that brings him worry and will cause him to dedicate his heart to His love, his tongue to His remembrance, and his limbs to His obedience.

92

Of the greatest torments in the worldly life is disunity and discord of the heart, and poverty being always in front of the eyes of the servant, never leaving him. If it was not for the drunkenness of the lovers of the worldly life, they would have called out for help from this torment.

93

The lover of the worldly life is never freed from three things: A haunting sorrow, constant tiredness, and a regret that never ends, because its lover does not acquire any of it except that his ego desires something more, as in the saying of the Prophet: "If the child of Adam had two valleys filled with wealth, he would seek a third". One of the pious predecessors is recorded as saying: "Whoever loves the worldly life, then let him accustom himself to bearing afflictions."

94

Who is the one who is afflicted with the love of images [i.e. love of the illusory things of the worldly life]? Only hearts that are empty of the love of God and sincerity toward Him are so afflicted, for the heart cannot help but become attached to something that it loves. Whoever does not make God alone his beloved, his Lord and his Worshiped, then his heart will inevitably become attached to something else.

95

Of the plots of Satan: He commands you to meet the poor and the needy with a scowl and to not see them as humans.

96

He has no need for their obedience toward His commands, for He is the Needless, the Praiseworthy, and He has no stinginess toward them when He forbids them from what He has forbidden them, for He is the Most Giving, the Most Gracious. Of His mercy is that He reduces the worldly life for them and clouds it in their eyes so that they do not take comfort in it and do not put their trust in it, so that they put their desire in the eternal bliss in His home and by His side. And of His mercy is that He warns them about Himself, so that they do not become deceived about Him by treating Him in an unfitting manner.

97

Satan refused to prostrate to Adam to escape from humbling himself before him, and in this way he sought to glorify himself, so God made him the lowest and basest of all. In the same way, the worshipers of statues arrogantly refused to follow a human messenger, and to worship One God, and were well pleased to worship gods made of stone. Whoever refuses to humble himself before God or to spend his money in the way of His pleasure or to tire his spirit and his body in His obedience, it is inevitable that he will be made humble to something else and he will spend his money toward it, and he will tire his spirit and body in its obedience as a punishment for him.

98

A group has said: To patiently restrain oneself from sinning is better [than doing good deeds], since it is more difficult. Good deeds are done by both righteous and wicked people, but only the sincere in faith abstain from sinning. They said that abandoning what one's ego loves is evidence that the person for which it was abandoned is more beloved that one's own self and desires, as opposed to doing what someone loves, which does not necessarily mean that the person is more beloved to us than ourselves.

99

Whoever makes it a habit to perform deeds for the sake of God finds nothing harder than performing deeds for the sake of other than Him, and whoever makes it a habit to perform deeds for the sake of his desires and his own fortune finds nothing harder than performing deeds with sincerity and for the sake of God. This is true in all categories of deeds; a person who always spends in the way of God finds it difficult to spend in the way of other than Him, and vice versa.

100

Proudly showing off one's knowledge is worse in the sight of God than showing off one's wealth and lineage, for such a person would be using a means of the afterlife for a worldly purpose, while the possessor of wealth and lineage is only using worldly means for a worldly purpose.

101

One of the pious predecessors has been recorded as saying: "When Satan and his soldiers gather, there is nothing that pleases them as much as three things: A believer killing another believer; a man dying in a state of disbelief; and a heart that fears poverty".

102

The torment of being screened off from the Lord of the Worlds is one of the most severe types of torment that He uses on His enemies, as He says: "Therefore they will be screened off from their Lord that day." [Quran 83:15]

103

Whoever loves something other than God for the sake of other than God, its harm will be greater than its benefit, and its torment will be greater than the pleasure it brings.

104

All the names of the Lord, glory to Him, are beautiful names and there are no evil names among them, and all His attributes are attributes of perfection and there are no flawed attributes among them, and all His deeds are out of wisdom and there are no deeds among them that are empty of wisdom and benefit.

105

When God wants good for a servant, He removes his heart's ability to see his own good deeds, and he removes the ability of his tongue to talk about them. He busies him with seeing his sins, so that they are always in front of his eyes until he enters Paradise.

106

How blessed is the one who is too concerned with his own faults to concern himself with the faults of others! And how accursed is the one who forgets his own faults and busies himself with faults of the people!

107

The servant, from the moment he puts foot in this world, is on a journey toward his Lord, and the duration of the journey is the duration of the lifetime given to him.

108

Asceticism is not to give up worldly things with your hands while it still occupies your heart. Asceticism is to give it up with your heart while it is still in your hands, and this was the state of the Rashidun caliphs and ʿUmar bin ʿAbd al-ʿAzīz, about whose asceticism stories are told, even though the treasuries of the kingdom were under his command, and the state of the best of mankind [the Prophet Muhammad peace and blessings of God upon him], for whom God opened of the worldly life what He opened, but it only increased him in asceticism.

109

Of the most harmful things to the servant are his idleness and leisure, for the ego is never idle, if you do not busy it with that which benefits it, you will inevitably busy it with that which harms it.

110

The best that a servant can ask of the Lord, glory to Him, is His help toward doing what pleases Him. This is what the Prophet, peace and blessings of God be upon him, taught Muʿādh bin Jabal when he said: "O Muʿādh, by God I love you, so do not forget to say after every prayer: O Allah, help me in Your remembrance, gratitude toward You and worshiping You in the best manner possible".

III

Do not think that all blessings are given due to the honor of the servant in God's eyes, nor think that when God withholds something it is because of the low status of the servant in His eyes; rather, both His generosity and His withholding are afflictions and tests with which He tests His servants.

112

Whoever refuses to work for the sake of God alone, God afflicts him with having to work for the sake of the creation. The servant turns his back on working for the One in Whose hands is his harm, benefit, death, life and happiness, so he is afflicted with working for someone who has none of those powers toward him. In the same way, a person who refuses to spend in the way of God is afflicted with being forced to spend his money in the way of something else.

113

Whoever thinks well of himself is the most ignorant of people regarding himself, for thinking well of oneself prevents one from properly inspecting oneself; he becomes confused and sees his bad attributes as good ones and his flaws as perfections.

114

When a servant is pleased with his worship, it is a sign that he thinks well of himself, and that he is ignorant toward true servitude, and that he does not know what befits the Lord, glory to Him, and the proper way to treat Him.

115

The people of insight are most eager to seek forgiveness right after doing acts of worship, because of the shortcomings they see in their worship.

116

When a sin causes someone to feel glad, it is a sign of the strength of their desire for it, their ignorance of the status of the One they disobeyed, and their ignorance of its dangers and evil consequences.

117

A believer never attains perfect pleasure from a sin, and he cannot attain happiness through it. Sorrow will always be the constant companion of his heart whenever he tries to attain pleasure or happiness through a sin.

118

The truly enlightened one is the one whose good deeds appear small before his eyes, and his sins appear great to him. You increase in the sight of God by the amount that your deeds appear small to you, and whenever you consider yourself great and high in status in your heart, you become small in the sight of God.

119

The servant is always walking, never stopping; either upward, downward, forward or backward. Stopping does not exist in nature, nor in Islamic law. [Life] is entirely made up of stages that are passed at great speed, either toward Paradise or toward the Hellfire. Some walk fast, others slowly, some are ahead and others lag behind. No one stands still on the road.

120

Immediate repentance from a sin is obligatory and it is not permitted to delay it, and whenever it is delayed, this delay is disobedience toward God.

121

True repentance requires one to flee from the sin, to feel remorse, and to resolve to not return to it.

122

If the servant follows his desire, his opinions and views become corrupted so that he sees goodness where there is ugliness and ugliness where there is goodness, so that he confuses the truth for falsehood.

123

It is enough for the reduction of one's expectations in the worldly life [to read] these sayings of God: "Do you think, if We let them enjoy themselves for years, and then what they were promised comes to them, that what they enjoyed will be of any use to them?" [Quran 26:205-207], "On the day We gather them together—when it will seem as if they had tarried no more than an hour of a single day being introduced to one another" [Quran 10:45], "On the Day they see it, it will be as if they had only lingered for the evening or the morning of a single day." [Quran 79:46], "They will say, 'We tarried there for a day or part of a day. Ask those able to count!' He will say, 'You only tarried there for a little while if you did but know!'" [Quran 23:113-114], "On the Day they see what they were promised, it will be as if they had only tarried for just one hour of a single day. It has been transmitted! Will any be destroyed except for deviant people?" [Quran 46:35], "they will whisper secretly to one another, 'You only stayed [in the worldly life] for ten.' We know best what they will say when the most correct of them will say, 'You only stayed a day.'" [Quran 20:103-104]

124

Whenever the servant thinks the best of God, sincerely puts his hope in God and relies on Him, then God will never let him down.

125

Imam Aḥmad bin Ḥanbal says: "Asceticism has three ranks: The first is to abstain from what is forbidden, and this is the asceticism of the average believer. The second rank is to abstain from excess in what is permitted, and this is the asceticism of extraordinary believers. The third is to abstain from everything that distracts one from God, and this is the asceticism of the enlightened believers."

126

Whoever does not seek God will seek other than Him; whoever does not dedicate his heart to worshiping Him will worship other than Him; and whoever does not do his deeds for the sake of God will inevitably have to do them for the sake of other than Him.

127

Imam Aḥmad, may God have mercy on him, said: "People's need for knowledge is greater than their need for food and drink, since a person needs food and drink a few times a day, while he needs knowledge with every breath he takes".

128

The true man is the one who fears the death of his heart, not the death of his body. Most people fear the death of their bodies and are not concerned with the death of their hearts. They do not know of life except the material part of it.

129

Of the signs of the knower of God are that he does not make demands, he does not quarrel, he does not reproach, and he does not consider himself above anyone else, and he does not think that he has any rights over anyone else. And of his other signs: He does not grieve over a good thing that he misses, and he does not celebrate an evil thing that misses him, because he looks at things from the point of view of passing away and evanescence, for in truth everything [in this worldly life] is like a shadow or illusion.

130

When God wants good for His servant, He purifies him from every base and evil ingredient before he dies. He purifies him through His enabling him to repent with sincere repentance, to do good deeds that wipe out his sinful deeds and through hardships that cause the same, until he is able to meet God without having any sins to burden him.

131

"To God we belong and to Him we return" [Quran 2:156] is one of the best cures for afflictions, both in the short term and the long term, for it contains two important principles that if the servant succeeds in recognizing, he attains rest and freedom from his affliction. The first one is that the servant, his family and his wealth are all in reality God's property, lent to him by God, so that when He takes them, He is only taking back His property from the borrower. The second is that the fate and destiny of a person end up toward God, his true Master; he will inevitably leave the worldly life behind and come before his Lord alone, as He created him first, without family, wealth or tribe, but with his good and bad deeds. Thus if this is the servant's beginning, present state and end, how can he be pleased with what he has, or grieve over what he has lost?

132

There are two types of love. One of them is a Paradise in this worldly life, a cause for the soul's gladness, the heart's pleasure and the bliss, nourishment and cure of the spirit, and its very livelihood and cause for joy, and that is the love of God alone in the heart. And there is a love that is torment for the soul, sorrow for the spirit, a prison for the heart, and a constriction of one's breast, a cause for pain, toil and suffering, and that is the love of other than God, glory to Him.

133

Know with certainty that the formal prayer is the joy of the heart of the lovers [of God], and pleasure of their souls, and the garden of the worshipers and the pleasure of the spirits of the ones who fear God, the criterion for measuring the state of the sincere ones, the gauge for determining the state of the seekers, and God's mercy that He has bestowed upon His believing servants.

134

As long as the servant carries out the remembrance of God and strives toward Him, God's mercy pours upon him like a torrential rain. But if he becomes heedless, he will suffer drought because of it, and if he is overcome by heedlessness and taken over by it, his land becomes a dead and ruined land, his year becomes a barren and dry year, and the fire of desires blows everywhere over it like simoom [hot, dry and dusty desert wind].

135

The formal prayer was established so that the servant uses all of his limbs in worship along with his heart.

136

[When the servant says "God is great" during the formal prayer, it means that] God is greater in his heart than anything else. He makes this statement true in his heart by not having anything greater than God in his heart that would distract him from Him. If his heart contains something that distracts him from God, it is evidence that that thing is greater to him than God. If he is distracted from God by something else, the thing that distracts him is more important to him than God, and his saying of "God is great" is only by the tongue, not the heart.

137

Ibn Taymīya, may God have mercy on him, said to me: "If a sheepdog tries to attack you, do not busy yourself with trying to fight it back. Rather, ask the shepherd for help and he will remove the dog. And when the servant seeks refuge in God from Satan, He will protect him from him."

138

Whoever tastes the joy of true prayer knows that the saying of "God is great" and the recitation of al-Fātiḥa cannot be substituted by anything else, and knows that nothing can substitute for carrying out standing in prayer, bowing and prostrating, because each one of them contains a secret, an effect and a type of worship that other things do not contain, and every verse of al-Fātiḥa contains a type of worship and joy that is special to it and that cannot be found in anything else.

139

To truly enjoy the benefits of worshiping God through bowing in prayer, the servant has to consider himself small and insignificant before his Lord, so that this feeling of insignificance removes from his heart any arrogance and self-glorification he has, or any glorification he has toward the rest of the creation, so that it is replaced by the glorification of God alone without partner. The servant praises God through this by lowering himself before Him, bowing his head, bending his back, and speaking words of praise and glorification about Him.

140

The Prophet said "give us rest through prayer"[13], rather than saying "give us rest from prayer", the way the person who considers it a burden would say, who does not perform it except by going against his own will and forcing himself to do it, who feels tormented while doing it, and when he is done with it, he feels his heart and spirit freed. That is because his heart is filled with other than Him, and the prayer keeps him away from the worldly things he loves and is attached to, and thus the prayer feels like torment for him until it ends. This is apparent in the state of the one who hurries the prayer while his heart is facing away from his Lord, who has abandoned taking refuge in it and performing it with fear and trembling in his heart, so he performs it, knowing that there is no way of avoiding it, but in a very deficient way, saying with his tongue what is not in his heart, and with his heart saying "if only the

---

[13] Spoken to one of his Companions to initiate the prayer.

prayer would be over so that I can get some rest from it", rather than saying "so that I can get some rest [and peace of mind] through it".

141

God, glory to Him, wanted to take among the children of Adam prophets, messengers, friends and martyrs, loved by Him and loving toward Him. Therefore He withdrew Himself from them to let them deal with His enemies on their own, in this way testing them. When they preferred Him and strove with their souls and wealth in His way, they earned His love and approval and closeness to Him, which would have been impossible to earn without this process [of testing]. The ranks of messenger-hood, prophecy, martyrdom and love and dislike for His sake and showing friendship toward His friends and enmity toward His enemies are of the greatest ranks which could not have been earned except in the way that God had arranged through lowering [Adam] to the earth and making his livelihood and the livelihood of his offspring in it.

142

God, glory to Him, is the possessor of the Beautiful Names; of His names are the Forgiving, the Merciful, the Pardoning, the Abaser, the Exalter, the Giver of Honor, the Giver of Humiliation, the Enlivener, the Causer of Death, the Inheritor and the Patient. God wishes His attributes to become manifest, so in His wisdom He decided to send Adam and his offspring down to a home in which the effects of His Names become manifest to them. He forgives, shows mercy, exalts, gives greatness, lowers, abases and takes vengeance from whomever He wills, and He withholds and gives freely, and all the other ways in which His Names and Attributes become manifest.

143

God, glory to Him, sent [humanity] down to a home where their belief in God has to be without having seen Him. Faith without seeing is true faith. As for faith after seeing, everyone on the Day of Judgment will have it, but their faith will have no benefit except those who also had faith in the worldly life. Had they been created in the home of Bliss [Paradise], they wouldn't have acquired the rank of faith without seeing. The pleasure and grace that is earned through this cannot be earned otherwise.

144

God, glory to Him, "when He said to the angels: 'I am putting a steward [agent or deputy] on the earth,' they said, 'Why put on it one who will cause corruption on it and shed blood when we glorify You with praise and proclaim Your purity?'" [Quran 2:30] He replied by saying: "I know that which you do not know" [Quran 2:30]. He then showed His knowledge to His servants and angels of what He had caused to exist on earth of the attributes of His creation, His prophets, His friends and those who strive toward Him by doing what He loves and pleases while struggling against their own lusts and desires, leaving what they love to increase their closeness to Him.

145

God, glory to Him, loves the patient, the good-doers, those who fight in His way, those who repent, those who purify themselves, and those who show gratitude toward Him. [...] In His wisdom, He decided to cause Adam and his offspring to take up residence in a home where they would have the opportunity to show these attributes through which they would acquire the highest ranks of His love, therefore His banishing them to earth was of His greatest blessings to them, "God selects for His mercy whomever He wills. God's favor is truly vast." [Quran 2:105]

146

God, glory to Him, created His creation to worship Him, and that is their purpose, as He says: "I have not created the jinn and humans except to worship Me" [Quran 51:56]. It is clear that the perfect servitude and worship that is required of humans cannot be achieved in the Home of Bliss [Paradise], but can only be achieved in the home of affliction and trials.

147

True love [toward God] is that which is stable regardless of obstacles, opposing forces and causes for separation. As for the love that is conditional upon good health, bliss, pleasure and getting what one desires from the beloved, that is not a true love and has no constancy.

148

'Abd-Allāh ibn 'Abbās says: "God has made it obligatory upon Himself toward the person who reads the Quran and acts by it to never let him go astray in this world and to protect him from torment and ruin in the Hereafter."

149

God, glory to Him, commanded His Prophet to pray to Him for increase in knowledge, saying: "Exalted then be God, the true King; and do not try to anticipate the Quran before the completion of its revelation, but pray: 'O Lord, give me greater knowledge.'". This is enough honor for knowledge, that He commanded His Prophet to ask Him for more of it.

150

Ibn Masʿūd, may God be pleased with him, says: "Knowledge is sufficient to cause the fear of God, and ignorance is enough to be arrogantly deceived about God".

151

God, glory to Him, says: "Remember the blessings and favors of God so that you may be successful" [Quran 7:69] Thus the remembrance of His favors and blessings upon His servants, glory to Him, are a cause for success and happiness since doing so increases one's love, gratitude and obedience toward Him and enables him to see how much shortcoming there is in his performance of the deeds that He has made obligatory upon him.

152

If repentance had not been one of the most beloved things to God, He would not have tested one of the most honored of His creations [humans] with sins. Repentance is the pinnacle of human perfection.

153

God shows His servant the extent of His forbearance and grace in the way He hides his faults and sins. Had He wished He would have quickened his punishment and would have dishonored him among His servants so that his life among them would have become bitter. But instead He honors him by covering his shortcomings. He covers him through His forbearance and provides for him protective measures even while he is sinning, to protect his dignity.

154

Be to God as He wishes, and He will be to you more than you can wish for.

155

This world is a bridge and a bridge should not be taken as a home.

156

O you who sold yourself for the sake of something that will cause you suffering and pain, and which will also lose its beauty, you sold the most precious item for the cheapest price, as if you neither knew the value of the goods nor the meanness of the price. Wait until you come on the Day of mutual loss and gain and you will discover the injustice of this contract.

157

O you who are patient! Bear a little more... just a little more remains.

158

Satan rejoiced when Adam came out of Paradise, but he did not know that when a diver sinks into the sea, he collects pearls then rises again.

159

I was told of a man from the Children of Israel who had a need that he wanted fulfilled by God. So, he engaged in constant worship and then asked God for his need.

When he did not see that his need was fulfilled, he spent the night blaming himself, saying: "O self! What is wrong with you that is preventing your need from being fulfilled?"

And he spent the night sad and holding himself to account, saying: "By God, the problem is not with my Lord. Rather, the problem is with myself," and he remained in such a state of holding himself responsible until his need was finally taken care of.

160

This worldly life is like a shadow. If you try to catch it, you will never be able to do so. If you turn your back towards it, it has no choice but to follow you.

161

When you make supplication, it is a sign that God loves you and has intended Good for you.

162

If a person loves an attribute of God, then this will help him to reach Him.

163

He who keeps knocking at a door is most likely to get the door opened or him. So keep knocking at the doors of the heavens.

164

If God wants good for a slave, He strips away from his heart the ability to see his own good deeds and speaking about them with his tongue, and preoccupies him with seeing his own sin, and it continues to remain in front of his eyes until he enters Paradise.

165

And if you reflect on most people's situation, you will find that they look at their rights over God and do not look at God's right over them, and from here is where they broke off from God.

166

When there is money in your hand and not in your heart, it will not harm you even if it is a lot; and when it is in your heart, it will harm you even if there is none in your hands.

167

If the heart is fed by love, the greed for pleasure would disappear.

168

By God, it is difficult for a person to know his own intentions for his deeds, so how can he possibly know with certainty the intentions of others?

169

The heart will rest and feel relief if it is settled with God, and it will worry and be anxious if it is settled with people.

170

Know that your need of God accepting your charity is infinitely greater than the need of the one to whom you give your charity.

171

Whoever is prevented from disobeying God by upholding the dignity of God in his heart, God will protect his dignity in the hearts of the creation and will prevent them from dishonoring him.

172

The key to the life of the heart lie in reflecting upon the Quran, being humble before God in secret, and leaving sins.

173

Whoever prefers God to all others, God will prefer him to others.

174

One of the most beneficial of remedies is persisting in supplication.

175

He created the seven seas, but what He loved was a tear from you [out of longing for Him] but your eyes were tearless.

176

Truly in the heart there is a void that cannot be removed except with the company of God Almighty. And in there is a sadness that cannot be removed except with the happiness of knowing God and being true to Him. And in there is an emptiness that cannot be filled except with love for Him and by turning to Him and always remembering Him. And if a person were given all of the world and what is in it, it would not fill this emptiness.

177

God does not close a door to his slave, out of wisdom, except that He opens two others to him.

178

When God tests you it is never to destroy you. When He removes something in your possession it is only in order to empty your hands for an even greater gift.

179

When a person spends his entire day with no concern but God alone, God will take care of all his needs and take care of all that is worrying him; He will empty his heart so that it will be filled only with love for Him.

180

Whoever has offended you and then approached you to apologize, humility obligates that you accept his apology whether it is truthful or not, and that you leave his secret thoughts to God. The sign of generosity and humility is that if you notice a defect in his apology, you do not address it nor hold it against him.

181

The people who have knowledge of God have agreed that sins done in solitude are the root of retrogression (going back to a life of sin), and that good deeds done in hiding are the greatest causes of steadfastness.

182

Sometimes, I have a certain need (that I wish to ask) God, so I ask Him earnestly. Then, I find that the door of dialogue opens up for me, and I recognize God more (I become more aware of Him), and feel humbled before Him, and feel a great sense of joy and happiness, due to which I prefer that the answer to my prayer be delayed, so that this joyous state may continue.

183

If it was not for the hardships of life the servant would have been afflicted by arrogance, self-worship, Pharoanic self-aggrandizement, and the hardness of the heart, which would have caused him to perish sooner or later.

Printed in Great Britain
by Amazon